D0386971

FREE, FEARLESS
FEMALE

WILD THOUGHTS ON WOMANHOOD

Willow Creek Press

Published by Willow Creek Press
P.O. Box 147, Minocqua, Wisconsin 54548

Editor/Design: Andrea K. Donner

Printed in Canada

Canada Lynx © Lisa & Mike Husar / TeamHusar.com

It is only rarely that one can see in a little boy the promise of a man, but one can almost always see in a little girl the threat of a woman.

Alexandre Dumas
(1802-1870) French novelist and playwright

Baby Elephant playing with mother's tail © Mitsuaki Iwago / MindenPictures.com

For most of history, Anonymous was a woman.

Virginia Woolf
(1882-1941) British writer

Virginia Woolf (née Stephen) was one of the most notable and prolific Modernist writers. Her feminist tract, *A Room of One's Own*, argues that women need education, a private room to work in, and enough money to live independently in order to write fiction. In this text, she creates an imaginary figure, Judith Shakespeare, William Shakespeare's sister, who "was as adventurous, as imaginative, as agog to see the world as he was," but because she was a woman was not able to pursue her genius. Woolf wrote nine novels, one play, over five volumes of essays, portraits, memoirs and reviews, more than fourteen volumes of diaries and letters, and forty-six short stories. She took her own life in 1941.

*I*f you want something said, ask a man.
If you want something done, ask a woman.

Margaret Thatcher
(1925-) Prime Minister of Great Britain

Margaret Thatcher's (née Roberts) political career has been one of the most remarkable of modern times. She became the first (and so far, the only) woman to lead a major Western democracy. She won three successive General Elections and served as British Prime Minister for more than eleven years (1979-1990), a record unmatched in the twentieth century.

Lioness attacking kudu prey © Martin Harvey / PeterArnold.com

*S*elf-reliance is the only road
to true freedom.

Patricia Sampson
U.S. writer

Patricia Sampson is the author of the book, *A Star to Steer By*, published in 1979.

Leaping Arctic Wolf © Jim Brandenburg / MindenPictures.com

F was always looking outside myself for strength and confidence, but it comes from within. It is there all the time.

Anna Freud
(1895-1982) Austrian psychoanalyst

Anna Freud was born in Vienna, Austria, the daughter of Sigmund Freud. She chaired the Vienna Psychoanalytic Society, and emigrated with her father to London in 1938, where she organized a residential war nursery for homeless children. She was a founder of child psychoanalysis.

*W*omen complain about premenstrual syndrome, but I think of it as the only time of the month I can be myself

Roseanne Barr
(1952-) U.S. comedienne

Roseanne Barr first earned recognition through her stand-up comedy routine, an act that came to life while she was working as a cocktail waitress. She started by cutting down men who made passes at her, and customers kept coming back for more. Barr spent several years performing at various venues where she honed her act, further concentrating on "funny womanness."

Badger © Denver Bryan / denverbryan.com

*F*If men menstruated, they would brag about how much and for how long.

Gloria Steinem
(1934-) U.S. writer, feminist, political activist

Gloria Steinem began a career as a freelance writer in 1960, when she earned both popular and critical notice with her 1963 article "I Was a Playboy Bunny," published in *Show* magazine. In that piece, Steinem recounted her three-week experience working undercover as a waitress in a New York Playboy Club and exposed the low wages and poor working conditions to which she and her fellow "bunnies" were subjected. In 1972, she founded *Ms.* magazine, the first magazine to offer a woman's viewpoint on political, social, cultural, religious, and other issues.

King Penguins © Frans Lanting / MindenPictures.com

I see my body as an instrument, rather than an ornament.

Alanis Morissette
(1974-) Canadian singer

Alanis Morissette burst onto the American music scene in 1995 with her *Jagged Little Pill* album. The album sold more than thirty million copies around the world and became one of the most successful recordings in music history. In 1996, she received Grammys for Album of the Year and Rock Album, as well as Female Rock Vocal Performance and Rock Song of the Year for "You Oughta Know."

Graceful Crab © Mark Conlin / Larry Ulrich Stock Photography, Inc.

*A*ny woman who thinks the way to a man's heart is through his stomach is aiming about 10 inches too high.

Adrienne E. Gusoff
U.S. writer, lecturer, humorist

Adrienne E. Gusoff is a freelance writer, lecturer, humorist, and motivational speaker. For many years, she wrote the advice column for an international magazine, and is currently the advice columnist for an on-line e-zine. She speaks to singles groups throughout the New York City area and counsels private clients on relationship issues.

Chinstrap Penguins courtship © Frank S. Balthis

*F*I've never met a man who could look after me. I don't need a husband. I need a wife.

Joan Collins
(1933-) British actress

Joan Collins made her film debut in *Lady Godiva Rides Again* (1951) and used her sultry appeal and headline-catching private life to build a career as an international celebrity. Her career was revitalized with a leading role in the universally-popular television soap opera *Dynasty*. Married four times, she has written one volume of autobiography, *Past Imperfect*, and a novel, *Prime Time*. Her sister is the best-selling novelist Jackie Collins.

Mountain Gorillas © Adrian Warren / Ardea.com

$\mathcal{E}$ver notice that what the hell
is always the right decision?

Marilyn Monroe
(1926-1962) U.S. actress

Marilyn Monroe was born Norma Jean Mortenson and spent most of her childhood in foster homes or
an orphanage. Promoted as a slightly ditzy blonde exuding a breathless sexuality, she became famous
after starring in films such as *Bus Stop* and *Some Like It Hot*. On August 5, 1962, Monroe was found
dead of an overdose of barbiturates in her home in Los Angeles. After several years in which she was
discussed almost entirely in terms of a sex goddess, she came to be perceived as a symbol of the exploita-
tion of women by Hollywood and men in general.

Never bend your head. Hold it high. Look the world straight in the eye.

Helen Keller
(1880-1968) U.S. writer, lecturer

At the age of 19 months, Helen Keller was struck with a fever that left her blind and deaf. A devoted tutor, Anne Sullivan, taught Keller to read, write, and speak; and Keller spent the remainder of her life leading humanitarian efforts to vastly improve the quality of living for the disabled. Among her successes, she helped to eliminate the practice of institutionalizing the disabled. She received numerous national and international awards for her humanitarian efforts, including the Theodore Roosevelt Distinguished Service Medal, the distinguished service medal from the American Association of Workers for the Blind, the French Legion of Honor, and the Presidential Medal of Freedom.

*T*oughness doesn't have to come
in a pinstriped suit.

Dianne Feinstein
(1937-) U.S. Senator

Senator Dianne Feinstein was elected to the Senate in 1992 by 5,505,780 Californians, the most votes cast for a Senator in U.S. history. Her career has been one of firsts — she was the first woman on the San Francisco Board of Supervisors; the first woman Mayor of San Francisco; the first woman elected Senator of California; and the first woman member of the Senate Judiciary Committee.

Female Loggerhead Turtle returning to sea after laying eggs © Tom Blagden / Larry Ulrich Stock Photography, Inc.

*T*he thing women have got to learn is that nobody gives you power. You take it.

Roseanne Barr
(1952-) U.S. comedienne

The popular television show, *Roseanne*, starring Roseanne Barr, premiered in October of 1988, and almost single-handedly changed the face of situation comedy. Barr told *The New York Times*, "The show was about women, gender, politics, the working class. Did I think it would be successful? I actually did. Because I knew it was filling a void."

Praying Mantis in defensive display © Konrad Wothe / MindenPictures.com

I shall not sit down. I will not lose
my only chance to speak.

Susan B. Anthony
(1820-1906) U.S. suffragist

Susan B. Anthony said these words after being found guilty of civil disobedience, in 1873, for stepping into a voting booth and marking the ballot. Working all her life for women's rights, Anthony's exhaustive canvass of New York State's sixty voting districts has become a model for grassroots organizers for feminist causes. Her strategies helped the women's suffrage movement post its first victory in 1860 with the passage of a bill permitting women to control their own earnings and contracts, and to serve as the guardians of their children. Obtaining the right to vote, however, proved to be a far more difficult undertaking, and one which she did not see realized in her lifetime.

*F*If you want to sacrifice the admiration
of many men for the criticism of one,
go ahead, get married.

Katharine Hepburn
(1907-2003) U.S. actress

One of the silver screen's most unique and enduring personalities, Katherine Hepburn's career as a leading lady spanned seven decades, over fifty films, and a record twelve Oscar nominations (four wins). She was one of the first stars to take control of her career while still working within the confines of the studio system.

Bull and cow Elk © Frank S. Balthis

*I*f pregnancy were a book, they would cut the last two chapters.

Nora Ephron
(1941-) U.S. author, screenwriter, movie director

Nora Ephron co-wrote the screenplays *Silkwood*, *Cookie*, and *You've Got Mail*, and wrote the screenplays *Heartburn*, *When Harry Met Sally*, *My Blue Heaven*, and *Sleepless in Seattle*. She's also the author of several essay collections, including *Wallflowers at the Orgy*, *Crazy Salad: Some Things About Women*, *Scribble, Scribble: Notes on the Media*, and the autobiographical novel, *Heartburn*.

Very pregnant Dartmoor Pony © David Dixon / Ardea.com

37

Sometimes when I look at my children I say to myself, "Lillian, you should have stayed a virgin."

Lillian Carter, mother of Jimmy and Billy

Lillian Carter was a nurse who married James Earl Carter, a peanut farmer in Georgia. They had two sons, Jimmy and Billy. Jimmy became the 39th President of the United States (1977-1981). His efforts since his presidency to find peaceful solutions to international conflicts, to advance democracy and human rights, and to promote economic and social development earned him the Nobel Peace Prize in 2002.

African lioness snarling at playful cub © Denver Bryan / denverbryan.com

*D*eath and taxes and childbirth! There's
never a convenient time for any of them!

Margaret Mitchell
(1900-1949) U.S. writer

Margaret Mitchell is the author of the best-selling novel, *Gone With the Wind*. The book was published in 1937 and broke all previous publication records, selling 50,000 copies in one day and two million within a year. In addition to its staggering sales, the novel won both the Pulitzer Prize and the National Book Award in 1937. As of 1998, *Gone With the Wind* was the best-selling book of all time, after the Bible, with a total of 23 million copies sold worldwide.

41

*T*here must be quite a few things
a hot bath won't cure,
but I don't know many of them.

Sylvia Plath
(1932-1963) U.S. writer and poet

Sylvia Plath was an outstanding student who won a scholarship to Smith College and a Fulbright to England. She met and married poet Ted Hughes in 1956. Her first poetry collection, Colossus, was published in 1960 to favorable reviews. Plath gave birth to the couple's second child in 1962, the same year she discovered her husband was having an affair. He left the family to move in with his lover, and Plath desperately struggled against her own emotional turmoil and depression. She moved to London and wrote dozens of her best poems in the winter of 1962. With sick children, frozen pipes, and a severe case of depression, Plath took her own life in February 1963 at age 30.

43

*L*ife shrinks or expands in
proportion to one's courage.

Anaïs Nin
(1903-1977) French writer

Anaïs Nin established a publishing house in 1935, Siana Editions, because no one would publish her erotically charged works. She was discovered by the literary world in the 1960s, eventually becoming best-known for her series of intensely personal journals begun in 1931, *The Diary of Anaïs Nin* (10 volumes). She also wrote novels, short stories, and erotica, all clearly drawing on the contents of her journals.

Ring-tailed Lemur © Steve Bloom / stevebloom.com

*M*My favorite thing is to go
where I've never been.

Diane Arbus
(1923-1971) U.S. photographer

Diane Arbus (née Nemerov) operated a successful fashion photography studio for nearly 20 years before turning her eye to people on the fringes of society for which she became renowned. In the 1950s, she began to make an intimate record of people "without their masks," and photographed the unapproachable: transvestites, dwarves, prostitutes, nudists, and the everyday ugly. She committed suicide when she was 48 years old.

Polar Bear © Denver Bryan / denverbryan.com

I am not afraid of storms, for I am learning how to sail my ship.

Louisa May Alcott
(1832-1888) U.S. writer

Louisa May Alcott is most celebrated for her children's fiction, which includes the eight novels grouped under the *Little Women* series. Alcott is credited with being a pioneer in the creation of realistic fiction for children, depicting children as multi-dimensional, thinking individuals. Her novels also demonstrate many of her beliefs, including a belief in co-education and other educational reforms, and a feminism that supported the idea of self-dependence for women and criticized many of the social customs expected of them.

Macaroni Penguin © Steve Bloom / stevebloom.com

*F*I have no riches but my thoughts.
Yet these are wealth enough for me.

Sara Teasdale
(1884-1933) U.S. poet

Sara Teasdale's poetry was first published in 1907. She wrote several collections of poetry in the following decade and became known for the intensity of her lyrics. Expressing disenchantment with marriage, Teasdale's late poetry resonated with suffering and strength. According to one biographer, Sara Teasdale spoke for "women emerging from the humility of subservience into the pride of achievement."

*S*uccess is liking yourself,
liking what you do,
and liking how you do it.

Maya Angelou
(1928-) U.S. writer

Maya Angelou (née Marguerite Johnson) published her first book, *I Know Why The Caged Bird Sings*, in 1970, the story of the first 17 years of her life up until the birth of her son. The memoir was met with astonishing critical acclaim and popular success. Since then, Angelou has become one of the most celebrated writers in America and a distinctive voice of African-American culture in particular. She was nominated for a Pulitzer Prize in 1971 for her first volume of poetry, and has received over 50 honorary degrees at different institutions.

Red Fox © Lisa & Mike Husar / TeamHusar.com

*S*ome of my best leading men
have been dogs and horses.

Elizabeth Taylor
(1932-) U.S. actress

Elizabeth Taylor was born in England but moved to America as a young girl where she became a child star after acting in *National Velvet* in 1944. Generally considered to be one of the most beautiful women alive, Taylor earned an increased measure of critical respect as an actress in the 1950s, and was nominated for an Oscar three times during that decade. She has won two Academy Awards for Best Actress for her performances in *Butterfield 8* (1960) and *Who's Afraid of Virginia Woolf* (1966). In her later life, acting has taken a backseat to her pursuit of humanitarian causes, most notably AIDS research.

*W*hatever women do they must do twice as well as men to be thought half as good. Luckily, this is not difficult.

Charlotte Whitton
(1896-1975) Canadian politician

Charlotte Whitton was a children's advocate and politician who was elected Mayor of Ottawa in 1951. She was the first woman to become a mayor of a large Canadian city.

Red Fox bringing Arctic ground squirrels to pups © Jock Wilburn / AnimalsAnimals

F

I love being married. It's so great to find
that one special person you want
to annoy for the rest of your life.

Rita Rudner
(1956-) U.S. comedienne

Comedienne Rita Rudner has written three books, *Tickled Pink*, *Naked Beneath My Clothes*, and *Rita Rudner's Guide to Men*. Her first solo HBO special, "Rita Rudner's One Night Stand," was nominated for two Ace Awards.

Panthera Tigers © Martin Harvey / PeterArnold.com

I am extraordinarily patient, provided
I get my own way in the end.

Margaret Thatcher
(1925-) Prime Minister of Great Britain

During Margaret Thatcher's term of office she reshaped almost every aspect of British politics, reviving the economy, reforming outdated institutions, and reinvigorating the nation's foreign policy. For the last quarter century, Margaret Thatcher has been one of the world's most influential and respected political leaders, as well as one of the most controversial, dynamic, and plain-spoken.

Leopard © Denver Bryan / denverbryan.com

*S*elf-development is a higher
duty than self-sacrifice.

Elizabeth Cady Stanton
(1815-1902) U.S. suffragist

Elizabeth Cady Stanton, women's rights activist, editor, and non-fiction writer, was one of the most influential figures in the women's suffrage movement in the nineteenth century. Outspoken, energetic, and controversial, she aroused strong feelings in both her friends and enemies. She lived in a time when women could not own property, had no right to her earned wages, could legally be beaten by her husband, and had no legal rights over her children. With Lucretia Mott, she organized the first Women's Rights Convention in Seneca Falls, New York, in 1848, and spent the next fifty years organizing and articulating the campaign for women's equality.

Atlantic Loggerhead Turtle hatchling © Lynda Richardson / PeterArnold.com

Surviving is important,
but thriving is elegant.

Maya Angelou
(1928-) U.S. writer

Maya Angelou is hailed as one of the great voices of contemporary literature. As a poet, educator, historian, best-selling author, actress, playwright, civil-rights activist, producer and director, she continues to travel the world, spreading her legendary wisdom.

Mountain Lion © Denver Bryan / denverbryan.com

Nobody can make you feel inferior without your consent.

Eleanor Roosevelt
(1884-1962) U.S. humanitarian; First Lady (1933-1945)

Eleanor Roosevelt's tremendous participation in twentieth century politics impacted widespread issues, including feminism and civil rights, public policy and social work, and international peace relationships with the United States. Always a champion of women's rights and independence, Eleanor became the first wife of a president to hold a press conference (throughout her tenure as first lady, she held more than 300 press conferences). Additionally, she allowed only female journalists to attend, and in this way, she pressured the largely male-staffed newspapers to hire female reporters. Throughout most of her adult life, she was known as one of the most admired and courageous women in the world.

Puma © Frank S. Balthis

*S*ome of us are becoming the men we wanted to marry.

Gloria Steinem
(1934-) U.S. writer, feminist, political activist

Along with founding *Ms. Magazine* in 1971, Gloria Steinem also helped organize the National Women's Political Caucus, the Women's Action Alliance, and the Coalition of Labor Union Women. She also established MS Foundation for Women, an organization dedicated to helping underprivileged women.

*T*he male is a domestic animal which
if treated with firmness, can be
trained to do most things.

Jilly Cooper
(1937-) British writer, journalist

Jilly Cooper (née Sallitt) produced a regular column for the *Sunday Times* (1969-82) and *The Mail on Sunday* (1982-87), and has written a number of general interest works, including *How To Stay Married, Jolly Marsupial,* and *Angels Rush In.* She's also written several novels.

N

Never go to bed mad.
Stay up and fight.

Phyllis Diller
(1917-) U.S. comedienne

Phyllis Diller (nee Driver) appeared as a contestant on Groucho Marx's game show You Bet Your Life in 1955. Her memorable performance on the show sparked the advent of her national exposure. In her monologues, Diller adopted the stage personality of a typical housewife and spoke of topics that affected American suburbia — kids, pets, neighbors, and even mothers-in-law. In addition to her comedic talents, Diller performed (under the pseudonym Dame Illya Pillya) as a solo pianist with over 100 symphony orchestras throughout America.

Hippos © Frans Lanting / MindenPictures.com

*A*ll marriages are happy. It's trying to live together afterwards that causes all the problems.

Shelly Winters
(1922-) U.S. actress

Shelly Winters trained as a stage actress in New York City before her film debut in *What A Woman*. She won Supporting Actress Oscars for *The Diary of Anne Frank* (1959) and *A Patch of Blue* (1965).

Lions © Lisa & Mike Husar / TeamHusar.com

*P*eople call me a feminist whenever
I express sentiments that differentiate me
from a doormat or a prostitute.

Rebecca West
(1892-1983) British novelist and critic

Dame Rebecca West (pseudonym of Cicily Isabel Andrews, née Fairfield) was for a short time an actress, and took the name Rebecca West from the character she played in Ibsen's *Rosmersholm*. She is best known for her studies arising out of the Nuremberg war trials: *The Meaning of Treason* (1949) and *A Train of Powder* (1955). She had a son, the critic and author Anthony West (1914-87), with H.G. Wells. She was made a dame in 1959.

Snarling Lioness with pride © Mitsuaki Iwago / MindenPictures.com

*T*o ask women to become unnaturally thin
is to ask them to relinquish their sexuality.

Naomi Wolf
(1962-) U.S. author and feminist

Naomi Wolf's bestseller, *The Beauty Myth*, challenged the cosmetics industry and the marketing of unrealistic standards of beauty, launching a new wave of feminism in the early 1990s. *The New York Times* called it one of the most important books of the twentieth century. A graduate of Yale and former Rhodes Scholar, Wolf has written essays for *The New Republic*, *The Wall Street Journal*, *Glamour* and *The New York Times*. She was named by *TIME* as one of the 50 most notable leaders under age 40.

*F*I have no regrets.
Regret only makes wrinkles.

Sophia Loren
(1934-) Italian actress

Sophia Loren created an indelible image as the quintessential international sex symbol with her luminous beauty and magnetic screen presence. In an age that both adored and exploited beautiful women, Loren was one of the first foreign-language stars ever to attain a level of international success comparable to America's most popular domestic talents. She earned an Academy Award for Best Actress in 1961 for her role in *La Ciociara (Two Women)*. To date, she holds the notable distinction of being the only actress to win top honors for a foreign language film.

Chimpanzee © John Daniels / Ardea.com

*F*emale friendships that work are relationships in which women help each other belong to themselves.

Louise Bernikow
U.S. author

Louise Bernikow is the author of several books, including *The American Women's Almanac: An Inspiring and Irreverent Women's History*, and *Bark If You Love Me: A Woman-Meets-Dog Story*.

Hamadryas Baboon females grooming © J&P Wegner / AnimalsAnimals

83

_Y_ou grow up the day you have your first real laugh — at yourself.

Ethel Barrymore
(1879-1959) U.S. actress

Ethel Barrymore began acting almost as soon as she could talk. She and her brothers, Lionel and John, all became leading theatrical and film stars. As an actress on Broadway, Ethel was one of the legends of her generation. Her physical beauty and her regal bearing did much to promote the image of the Barrymores as the "royal family" of the U.S. stage and screen. The term "glamour girl" was invented specifically in reference to her.

Gray Seal © Anita M. Weiner

If you always do what interests you,
at least one person is pleased.

Katharine Hepburn
(1907-2003) U.S. actress

Katharine Hepburn's many film roles include *Guess Who's Coming To Dinner?*, *The African Queen*, *Long Day's Journey Into Night*, and *A Lion in Winter*. She was awarded an unprecedented four Academy Awards for Best Actress, the last being earned when she was 74 years old for her performance in the sentimental drama *On Golden Pond*.

Giant Panda © Lisa & Mike Husar / TeamHusar.com

*D*o you really have to be the ice queen
intellectual or the slut whore?
Isn't there some way to be both?

Susan Sarandon
(1946-) U.S. actress

Susan Sarandon's (nee Tomaling) film roles increased in quality and variety as she came into middle age.
She was nominated for three Academy Awards for Best Actress (*Atlantic City*, *Thelma and Louise*,
Lorenzo's Oil) before finally winning the award for *Dead Man Walking* in 1995. She and her partner,
Tim Robbins, are active in numerous political, cultural, and health causes.

Bobcat © Lisa & Mike Husar / TeamHusar.com

Until you've lost your reputation, you never realize what a burden it was.

Margaret Mitchell
(1900-1949) U.S. author

Margaret Mitchell was born in Atlanta, Georgia, where she began working as a journalist and feature writer (using the name Peggy Mitchell) for *The Atlanta Journal*. She married in 1925, but shocked Atlanta society by keeping her own name professionally. (In private life, she was known as Peggy Marsh.)

Mountain Gorillas mating © Gail Shumway / Bruce Coleman, Inc.

Too much of a good thing is wonderful.

Mae West
(1893-1980) U.S. actress, writer

Mae West was singing and dancing in amateur performances and winning local talent shows by the age of seven. While still a teenager, she became a star on the vaudeville stage, and soon became known for her flashy and tight-fitting clothing as well as her provocative comments, delivered in dialects or a throaty voice. Her costumes would typically include an assortment of rhinestones, leopard skins, and huge plumed hats, all worn on her five-foot-tall body. West wrote many plays, screenplays, and worked in the entertainment business until she was in her eighties.

Elephant Seal in kelp © Frank S. Balthis

Everyone's entitled to my opinion.

Madonna
(1958-) U.S. singer

Madonna gained popularity and stirred the pop music scene in the early 1980s. Known for her provocative stage and video performances, her bold attitude, and her somewhat ambiguous expression of a new feminism in her combination of sexuality and shrewdness, she was arguably the best-known woman in the world at the height of her popularity.

*D*on't compromise yourself.
You are all you've got.

Janis Joplin
(1943-1970) U.S. rock singer   -

Janis Joplin found her place among the counterculture of the 1960s, singing blues in the clubs and coffeehouses of San Francisco and Venice Beach, while indulging in drugs and alcohol. Eventually, she joined an existing hard-rock band called Big Brother and the Holding Company. Joplin served as lead vocalist, achieving a fierce blues sound that was unprecedented by white female artists at the time. In 1968, Joplin left the group and went solo. Open about her use of drugs and alcohol, the 27-year-old singer was found dead of an accidental heroin overdose in 1970.

We turn not older with years, but newer every day.

Emily Dickinson
(1830-1886) U.S. poet

Emily Dickinson was born in Amherst, Massachusetts, and remained at home, unmarried, all her life. Between 1858 and 1866, Dickinson wrote more than 1,100 poems, full of aphorisms, paradoxes, off rhymes, and eccentric grammar. She gathered her poems into hand-written copies bound loosely with looped thread to make small packets. The packets were stored in an ebony box, and were later discovered by her sister-in-law after Emily's death. Only seven poems were published during her lifetime, and editors had altered them all.

Woodchuck © Lisa & Mike Husar / TeamHusar.com

*T*he more you praise and celebrate your life,
the more there is in life to celebrate.

Oprah Winfrey
(1954-) U.S. talk-show host, actress, producer

Oprah Winfrey began her career in radio and television broadcasting. *The Oprah Winfrey Show* was launched in 1986 as a nationally-syndicated program, and grossed $125 million by the end of its first year. Winfrey soon gained ownership of the program, drawing it under the control of her new production company, Harpo Productions. Along with her many accomplishments in broadcasting and acting, Winfrey is a dedicated activist for women's and children's rights.

Bottlenose Dolphin © Flip Nicklin / MindenPictures.com

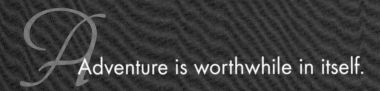

Adventure is worthwhile in itself.

Amelia Earhart
(1897-1937) U.S. aviator

Amelia Earhart first flew in 1920 and within a year made a solo flight. In 1928, she participated in a transatlantic flight with two men, becoming the first woman to fly the Atlantic. In 1932, flying solo, she set a transatlantic record of 14 hours, 56 minutes, and the following year she flew two more record-setting transatlantic flights. In 1937, she embarked on an equatorial world trip but ceased communications on July 2, shortly after leaving New Guinea. The plight of the aircraft has never been solved.

Cougar leaping © J&C Sohns / AnimalsAnimals

*O*h, never mind the fashion. When one has a style of one's own, it is always twenty times better.

Margaret Oliphant
(1828-1897) Scottish novelist

Margaret Oliphant (nee Wilson) wrote from an early age, but when she was widowed in 1859, she wrote from then on to support her own and her brother's children. Her first novel, *Mrs. Margaret Maitland*, began a prolific career in literature extending to more than 100 books and some 200 contributions to *Blackwood's Magazine*. She also wrote histories and biographies.

Snowy Egret © Lisa & Mike Husar / TeamHusar.com

At the worst, a house unkept cannot be so distressing as a life unlived.

Rose Macaulay
(1881-1958) British writer

Dame Rose Macaulay was a novelist, essayist, and poet. She won considerable reputation as a social satirist, with such novels as *Dangerous Ages* (1921). Her best-known novel is *The Towers of Trebizond* (1956). She was made a dame in 1958.

Woodchuck © Lisa & Mike Husar / TeamHusar.com

F used to think getting old was about vanity — but actually, it's about losing people you love. Getting wrinkles is trivial.

Joyce Carol Oates
(1938-) U.S. writer

Joyce Carol Oates' first successes as a writer came in her short stories. Her work is known for elements of random violence, the seedy underside of seemingly normal people, and descents into madness. She also writes novels, plays, and essays. Throughout her career, Oates has been honored with several literary prizes, including the O. Henry Special Award for Continuing Achievement, the Pushcart Prize, the Alan Swallow Award for fiction, the Bobst Award for Lifetime Achievement in Fiction, the Bram Stoker Lifetime Achievement Award for horror fiction, and the Fisk Fiction Prize.

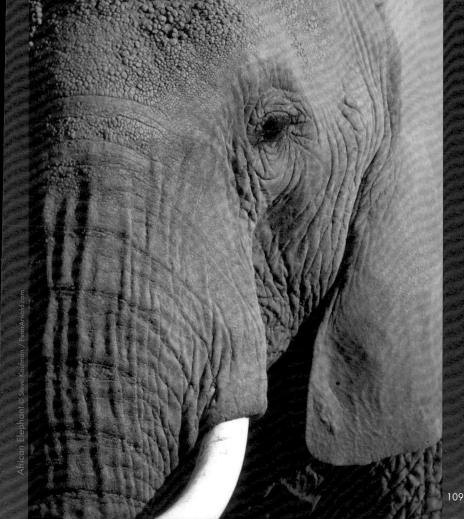

African Elephant © Steve Kaufman / PeterArnold.com

I prefer liberty to chains of diamonds.

Lady Mary Wortley Montagu
(1689-1762) British writer

Lady Mary Wortley Montagu (nee Pierrepont) was a poet and essayist, as well as a feminist, who gained a brilliant reputation among literary figures. While in Constantinople with her husband, she wrote her entertaining *Letters*, published in 1763 after her death, describing Eastern life. She also brought the small-pox inoculation from Turkey, introducing it to England, her own beauty having been marked by an attack while she was a young woman.